A NET TO CATCH THE WINDS,
AND OTHER POEMS

By the same author

A Net to Catch the Winds, and Other Poems

by
MAURICE LINDSAY

ROBERT HALE · LONDON

821
L IN

B

ISBN 0 7091 9482 X

Robert Hale Limited
Clerkenwell House
Clerkenwell Green
London EC1R 0HT

The publisher acknowledges the financial assistance of the
Scottish Arts Council in the publication of this volume

Photoset and printed in Great Britain by
Photobooks (Bristol) Limited
28 Midland Rd., St. Philips, Bristol
and bound by
Western Book Co. Ltd.

CONTENTS

PREFATORY NOTE

"All that a poet can do is warn," Wilfred Owen remarked. In making even that limited claim he was showing an optimism I find I cannot share. False and oppressive dogmas, foolish superstitions, tawdry values and uncountable and seemingly increasing examples of man's inhumanity to man leave one with the choice of tears or laughter. In my old age I have settled for the latter.

In these poems, many of them couched in light verse, the experiences I have "seized on", as Iain Crichton Smith once so accurately described my poetic process, are in some cases clearly personal, in others not. For the most part they deal with themes not previously explored in my *Collected Poems*, to which they therefore constitute a coda.

"The Ballad of the Hare and the Bassethound" was written for an anthology of verse for children edited by Alan Bold, "Hercules" as the answer to a challenge from my friend Charles Fraser. "Scotland the What?" first appeared anonymously in my anthology *Scottish Comic Verse*.

Few poets have dared to use the *ottava rima* stanza because of its strong association with Byron. I hope that in *A Net to Catch the Winds* I have handled it with sufficient competence and infused it with enough of myself to appease his lordship's ghost.

M.L.

Finally ...

GRANDCHILD VISITING
(for Carrie Leigh Barr)

She stands, her chubby knees gently swaying,
before the shapes on the television screen,
unaware of the hate the words are spraying,
or what the murdered falling bodies mean.

Through his own screams a baddie bites the floor.
The colours cease to hold her. *Look, here's me*,
the nosing basset saunters through the door;
and, innocent with love, she cries: "*Toe-bee*"!

CONDUCTORS
(for Sir Alexander Gibson)

Lines with the notes of music—meanings pointing
to distances we can't get to unaided
unless someone conducts us. Dictionaries
define *conduct* as "manage", "guide", "direct",
or "serve as a channel". We conduct ourselves
from place to place, and travel situations
we often wonder why we've reached. Conductors
in uniform are there for us to purchase
a piece of distance from, for us to use
with our own good or insufficient reasons.
Tall buildings, brittle in their fixed importance,
conduct unbolted lightning straight to earth

by circumventing their own distances.
But above others most to be revered,
conductors of music; subtle channellers
who give life back itself, mind out of time,
unfurling half-remembered hints of glory
to flap about our tattered human story.

THE SUM OF MOMENTS

A headless carcase slumped on a butcher's shoulder
from lorry to shop in a city's hungry street
sent me in mind to Orkney, years ago;
a dappled field of cows and a schoolboy dare.
Lie down, they said: *let the creatures lick your face.*

I lay sweet in that young grassy place:
the cows advanced, each through its own stare.
Their tongues roughly caressed my skin with a slow
assurance, till I leapt to my winner's feet,
and shadowed fearful time a moment colder.

DUSK IN A GLASGOW SQUARE

Darkness obliterates. Through spreading light
the street lamps press dried leaves. Their naked rustle
edges decay against the smell of night.
Kerbing low-geared, a cruise of cars hustle
each other round an empty office block
to pull up when the flash of booted thighs

flickers. A shadow peels out from the flock
leaning her whispered offer. The driver buys,
and revs off to the nearest parking lot.
Crouched in the crumpled scuffle of a seat,
he satisfies the need he thinks he's bought,
then runs her freshly back to her old beat.

Some father re-adjusts the dress of his disguises;
some daughter squares herself with what she realises.

NOCTURNE

In the middle of the night, the footless hours,
my fears take courage, crowd about my bed.
Leaning over me, the false breath
of their alarm chokes me. I rehearse
    the gasp of my own death.

In the morning, in the blood's awakening,
whey-faced, they slink away. A sunned-out moon
circles my living's dark side. Man again,
I wonder what it is they want of me:
    or rather, how, and when?

Lastly . . .

SPOKESPERSON'S APOLOGY

If we don't sell them stuff, then others will,
since self-defence has rights that none can shun,
and Britain must put money in her till.

Boys will be boys. Arms aren't sold to kill,
for Peace stares out the muzzle of a gun.
If we don't sell them stuff, then others will.

Who'd vote more tax to foot the nation's bill?
From such a notion politicians run;
yet Britain must put money in her till.

Flesh blasts apart, or cooks, a napalm grill;
most cools in bed, its thread of life unspun.
If we don't sell them stuff, then others will.

What does it matter how you round the hill
since priests affirm that Death has been undone,
and Britain must put money in her till?

There's no escape through logic's wordy skill:
fighting's the show with quite the longest run.
If we don't sell them stuff, then others will,
and Britain must put money in her till.

A PETITION FOR THE SAINTING OF
JOHN MacCUTTIT

Dear Holy Father, we, the faithful few
of Muckleshovit, heartfully assure you
that if of John MacCuttit's deeds you knew,
you'd dub him Blessed. So we put before you
for storage in your heavenly files, the claim
MacCuttit has to join those sainted brothers
whose days our diaries silently sustain.
He was a sharp one, noted above others
for spreading God's unquestionable teaching
that birth control's a sin. When passion shook him,
a Catholic vet, his hobby of lay preaching
increased and multiplied, then overtook him.

He'd practised Pauline abstinence between
begetting twenty kids in years as many,
although his conscience failed to intervene
when practising to turn an honest penny.
For daily to his neat suburban door—
his *clientèle* was rich and of the best—
came duchess, wife, trade unionist and whore,
each with a pussy that she wanted "dressed".

For years, without a thought of holy writ
set down to guide slow-multiplying savages,
this veterinary surgeon did commit
on stallions, bulls and cats subtracting ravages.
Believing sexual pleasure was a sin,
he justified his own by the contrition
of post-coital prayer. His kith and kin,
brute creatures, were not saved through this condition.

11

As Saul turned Paul upon the Tarsus road,
MacCuttit felt a throbbing, blind sensation—
halfway between the pub and home—explode,
pronouncing hungry death a Revelation.
No longer need he question who should feed
babies by millions dying of starvation.
The God of love meant *everything* to breed:
in breeding lay the clue to man's salvation.

At once this godly vet laid down his knives
and undertook no further operation
on hapless pussies, other than his wife's,
since that was in-the-family inflation—
a fault, Most Holy Father, looked at purely,
bestowing favours on a single woman
although she was his wedded wife. Yet surely
a secret sin or two makes saints more human?

The Muckleshovit cats now go and come,
like human males, on pleasure bent to sample.
The godly vet lies thinly in his tomb,
a monument to principled example.
Dear Holy Father, may the Great Assessor
approve of this petition, not rebut it,
so that five hundred years on, your successor
may sanctify the Blessed John MacCuttit.

HERCULES, or A TRIAL OF STRENGTH
(a moral fable for Charles Fraser, who provoked it)

I

When men were killing men with greater skill
than science had made possible before,
mass unemployment sapping human will,
the Pope pronouncing marriage best when frore,
and politicians, filled with dogma's lore,
proclaiming for our ills one choiceless cure—
strength through disaster; simple, safe and sure:

II

with ships, cars, fridges and much else—you name it—
there was a slump in paper lavatorial.
The trade grew doubly anxious. Can you blame it?
Had customs changed? Could creatures long sartorial
be copying their ancestors corporeal
who had no need of aids to basic cleanness?
Or was it just sheet-counting human meanness?

III

To reach the truth paid advertisers launched a
campaign to sell more paper through the telly.
With rigid rules Authority has staunched a
referral on the screen to functions smelly;
whatever happens underneath the belly
must be romanticised; a kind evasion
designed to ease reality's abrasion.

IV

So what more obvious then to import a
tame grizzly bear into the Hebrides,
its cuddly, close embrace a sure support, a
subliminal reminder of the sea's
perpetual cleansing action, sure to please
those who think creatures in captivity
much better off than wild from their nativity.

V

But Hercules—the bear was aptly named—
thought toughness quite unproved by toilet tissue.
During a rest-break, when no cameras aimed,
and eyes were fixed upon a call-girl's *fichu*
in *Playboy* or the like, this bear took issue
with human falsity, let out a roar
and ambled off to swim for Wiay's shore.

VI

His owner and the crew looked foolish downed men;
the telly news reported the betrayal.
How could a bear survive in straits that drowned men?
The local police said: "Anything you say'll
be taken down in evidence, so weigh all
your words." The swimming bear alone was speechless,
though also, as it seemed, mostly likely beachless.

VII

Islands were searched. One footprint gave a clue,
but no one found the foot that did the printing;
an aberration any one of you
out jogging might have cast with barefoot sprinting.
At last the telly newsmen took to hinting
that Hercules the bear must now have drowned
though, true, no washed-up body had been found.

VIII

But Hercules's owner, used to hugging
the profitable creature (and no wonder!)
dismissed such speculation, lightly shrugging
off theories that his bear had made a blunder.
With toilet rolls behind him none could sunder,
who'd be so foolish as to swim a length
of current-twisted seas beyond his strength?

IX

Days floated by. A murder here and there,
a child kidnapped, a sudden earthquake racking
some distant plot of earth, and soon the bear
was deemed newsworthless. No amount of jacking
the story up with rumour sadly lacking
a single fact could conjure out white rabbits
for journalists with empty-hatted habits.

X

One day a crofter ran back down his road
then, rooted, babbled of rewards, and how
across his field he'd "seen a bear, b'Goad!"
Nonsense, his friend said: *yon was chust a cow.*
The crofter burst out, furious by now:
*A cow has teats, a grizzly bear has fur
a tifference as plain as him from her.*

XI

The police set out upon their bicycles
and, sure enough, could soon confirm the sighting.
A thinner bear, his coat salted like icicles
felt hunger and the island wind's keen biting.
With advocaat and prawns they tried inviting
him to come quietly. Instead, he struck out,
despite his favourite meal, then once more struck out.

XII

A helicoptered vet with shadow flailing,
soon hovered over Hercules, and shot him
a tranquillizer! All was now plain sailing.
Inside a bundled net they quickly got him
and, sleeping, to his cage and owner brought him
back safely. News wires buzzed. *The bear's not dead.*
He's wakened with a slightly woozled head.

XIII

Bookings poured in. More advertisers sought him
for everything with which a bear connects.
For thousands down a TV station bought him
to take part in a quiz show. *He reflects*
great credit on us all, and the effects
of such bare courage must give inspiration,
a spokesman said, *throughout this faltered nation.*

XIV

What happened? Yes; more wars and rapes and lootings.
The bear grew rich, though couldn't use his money.
Upwards the sale of toilet rolls went shooting
(if reach-me-downs go "up"); a fact unfunny
to those who think all life's a flow of honey.
Who's left inside Moralitas's jail?
Each to his own end, wags this fable's tail.

BALLAD OF THE HARE AND THE BASSETHOUND
(for Carrie Leigh, Hanne and Rory)

The bassethound's a mournful fellow;
long ears that trail along the ground,
a baying voice that's like a cello,
a tail that circles round and round.

Yet bassethounds were bred for chasing,
through France's royal days of old,
the breathless hare, at first outpacing
the hound who, once he snuffed a hold

of the hare's scent, kept slowly clumbering
ditches, branches, burns and fields
till at the end of all his lumbering,
the limping hare, spring broken, yields.

We're civilised. So basset Billy,
his snuffling anchored to the ground,
was amiable, harmless, silly,
seeking for things he never found.

One sudden day he bumped his snout on
a lump of fur, a sleeping hare.
Poor Billy gazed with wrinkled doubt on
the creature that returned his stare.

At once the hare sent distance arcing
as towards the setting sun he sped,
while Billy sat upon his barking,
then turned and oppositely fled.

But not for long. The old blood-royal
that courses through a basset's veins
is not a thing for time to spoil,
even when it feeds slow-thinking brains.

His massive paws he pushed before him
and slithered to a skidding halt.
In vain did I command, implore him—
ancestral blood cried out "Assault!"

17

So yelping ancient doggy noises,
Billy set off in late pursuit.
Time waits for no such equipoises:
the jinking hare by then had put

two lengthy fields from where he started
and, smalling, breached a hill's horizon,
Billy, essentially kind-hearted,
pulled up with innocent surprise on

his wrinkled features. Body wagging,
he ambled back to where I waited.
With asking eyes he lay there sagging,
face saved and old French honour sated;

as if to say: "Come on now, praise me
for showing sense; en Français, *sens*;
like you, to kill's a thought dismays me,
so *honi soit qui mal y pense!*"

SCOTLAND THE WHAT?

Is Scotland a nation, or not?
is a question that troubles the Scot,
  since our banknotes and laws,
  our religion and tawse
don't add up to self-confident thought.

Where's the What for which Scots keep on yearning?
We strike when we ought to be earning;
  An Assembly! we shout,
  then vote the thing out
and get back to the business of girning.

Yet no matter how deeply one delves
through what history's stocked on our shelves,
   at least we still joke
   of the pig in the poke
we buy when we treat with ourselves.

TO CATCH THE LAST POST

The party's almost over. Though at times a
                             trifle odd,
I've thoroughly enjoyed it. Thank you for
                      having me, God.

And in Conclusion . . .

A NET TO CATCH THE WINDS

(A gratitudinal canter in light verse)

FOR JOYCE

Whispered leaves and lovers grassing,
gentleness there's no amassing,
music into silence tossing
   time rescinds.
Quick, poet, in the passing—
   a net to catch the winds!

1

Whatever fame you seek or rank aspire to,
or pleasures buy, conventional or odd,
there comes a moment when you can't conspire to
elasticate your tread from stiffened plod;
those weakened like Gerontius suspire to
the fancied shade of some constructed God
to spare their favoured souls oblivion's knife:
others, like me, just murmur: *Thank you, life!*

2

But gratitude's demands are more capacious
than to acquit a poet with one stanza,
his appetite for living still voracious.
What follows may in practice be just *sans* a
bare fact or two, but when the mode is spacious
wise readers know that poetry's bonanza
is never found constrained by what defines;
it's what emerges from between the lines.

3

Besides, throughout my life one keen ambition's
alone among the rest unsatisfied,
perhaps because my muse felt its conditions
too strict for any subject that she eyed,
doubting her rhymer's skill for such renditions:
throughout the years I've wished that I had tried
to write a poem in *ottava rima*,
which, were I English, I would rhyme with *schemer*.

4

But I'm not English; I'm a Glasgow Scot
born in what's now a Conservation Area
where laws control what you may do, what not.
For instance, woe betide you if you vary a
weathered saint, or plaster faceless rot;
you must replace them, even if there's nary a
public penny's help when you restore
what puffs and peels off like an ageing whore.

5

Those distant years ago when I appeared there
the place was in its prime, or so I'm told,
Rolls-Royces multiplying as you neared there;
but cars, like whores, mean nothing one day old;
your mother's milk is all that you revered there,
or nappy change when it was wet and cold:
unless, like dear Mackenzie, your recalling's
so total you still hear your infant bawlings.

6

My bandaged father lay somewhere in France,
wounded to silence in the Kaiser's war.
My mother ripened in an anxious trance,
uncertain if he'd see the child she bore.
But he was master of unlucky chance;
work, golf and war were games where one could score.
They said by fifty he'd not be alive;
he talked his vigorous way to eighty-five.

7

An uncle substituted for my father;
through boyhood years I was to him a son.
Until he died I found that I'd much rather
the substitute had been the real one.
Each Saturday, together we'd forgather,
and go exploring through comparison.
From him I learned the texture of the ways
a city shapes its huge anonymous days.

8

The kind of learning that I got at school
seemed dull when, after lying on my tummy
in a friend's house, aged twelve, against the rule
up late, the radio, as usual, crummy,
half-slipping under drowsiness's pull,
I suddenly sat upright on my bum be-
cause Haydn's music had enlarged the air,
sending delightful shivers everywhere.

9

O music! after love my first of pleasures;
dear joy! worth application's sacrifice,
enriching beyond speech with strains and measures
to substance feeling when the action dies;
for me like breath, not just a taste for leisure,
the worship that I gave you proved unwise.
At French I flopped, in mathematics fumbled;
The boy won't concentrate, my teachers grumbled.

10

Two other sirens whispered at my side.
With words of daily contact, Poetry's muse
murmured in sounds that sent a softening tide
of feelings, which as yet I couldn't use,
through me; but feelings that I wouldn't hide.
These or hard facts? I knew I had to choose.
The senses won. I chose to follow art;
which seemed the richer way, money apart.

11

The second muse from puberty's horizon
took, not surprisingly, the shape of girl.
No doubt today you wouldn't put a prize on
the she who set my thoughts in such a whirl.
Month after month she kept her childish guise on;
some husband later plucked her virtue's pearl,
for Nature scarce allowed us more than kiss,
me thirteen, she a breastless twelve-year miss.

12

Throughout my days to one thing I've held steady;
women were never inches in a tape.
My mother grew alarmed, though, when I said I
preferred a violin's to the female shape;
that was, until I saw a naked lady:
(what wonders lie concealed beneath a drape!)
Such posing young men hold to gain effect—
a sign of undeveloped intellect.

13

Meanwhile I slaved, when not engaged in schooling.
For hours I tackled Rode, Kreutzer, Spohr.
While other boys indulged in sport or fooling
with ogling girls, alone I'd practise more
thirds, sixths, arpeggios, octaves, double trilling
until my neck and finger-tips grew sore.
Imaged in self-love poor Narcissus drowned;
verse-making kept my thoughts on firmer ground.

14

Each Spring, proclaimed by trumpets daffodilled
in the Botanic Gardens while the tram
turning the Byres Road corner shrieked and shrilled,
I walked with Pope and pondered why I am,
a question which no obvious answer filled
that didn't smack of philosophic sham:
then, copying caesura and sensation,
I learned the poet's craft by imitation.

15

How else? From all that's past, the long connection
we can't escape's the blood of every one of us,
that ageless and incurable infection.
Whatever sallow youth thinks he'll have done of us
to give society a new complexion,
he's stuck at once with every mother's son of us:
unless he's homosexual or a hermit,
his stamping flesh endorses history's permit.

16

Then followed years when I was a Romantic.
There's few of us escape this lush complaint
since *Sturm und Drang*, with melancholic antic,
made subjectivity a cureless taint;
but cynicism, at its best semantic,
suspects the substance underneath the paint.
As well proclaim a faith in racial purity
as count on objectivity for surety!

17

Horse-drawn cabs to parties, yellow fogs,
cranes—flattened question-marks—above the river
seen from my bedroom window, crackled logs
and sherried aunts at Christmas—me, a sliver
of my found later self—were winter's cogs
turning a summer that I wished forever.
A paddle-steamer frothed us to the coast,
and all my searching fancy valued most.

18

Innellan opened gates of paradise;
glittering seas, the flush of flowers, and lawns
that slanted green with light, and the small eyes
of clouds floating blue days as halcyon's
a timeless fable; ships that passed like sighs,
their trailing foam wavelets that breathed anons
when ship and throb of churning screw had faded
into those distances that purpose traded.

19

The Clyde, it's true, was sometimes closed by mist
that clutched and clumped the Highland hills together,
and rain that shook the trees with angry fist;
but we forget the rages of rough weather,
remembering how honeysuckle kissed
after fresh showers, the wet caress of heather.
Since Nature's our one source of human healing,
no wonder poets find her so appealing!

20

But there now; I grow lyric, and digress.
The simple fact is, one can't live on scenery,
and men who calculate the more or less
of money, pour impatient scorn on greenery,
except, perhaps, when draped in halls to dress
up sales of work done by the local Deanery,
or Presbytery, if by chance your class
equates your superstitions with the mass.

21

One winter afternoon, walking a dog,
I climbed a hillock sloping off in scree.
A slip of gravel gave the beast a shog,
tumbling it downwards. By a stunted tree
it found its feet. Proud as a demagogue
it stood there watching as, on hand and knee,
I slithered past it, fracturing a scaefoid;
of doggy gratitude it was, I'd say, void.

22

That brought a tacit end to violin playing
and saved me fiddling in some third-rate band.
It saved me, too, from soldierly affraying—
a thing I doubted if my nerves could stand.
I heard a board of doctors sternly saying
what proved a most relieving reprimand:
Your right hand doesn't have its full mobility;
you lack the fighting man's complete agility.

23

I was, of course, no cowardly escaper,
having resigned myself to killing's chance;
now, I commanded only bits of paper
that balanced options, figures, facts and plans;
of others' deaths unwittingly a shaper,
saved from their hell by comic circumstance.
Few men aspire to die as martyred stoics.
Necessity's the mother of heroics.

24

But back again to love. My next attack of it
I suffered when a student with no money,
that sesame which gives a man the knack of it;
a pianist, sweet-faced, by temper sunny,
her play was such that once I'd seen the back of it,
my pricked idealism seemed quite funny.
She found dissecting sheep a better bet
than Mozart; so she married with a vet.

25

Lucky in love the third time (and I shout of it),
I've been a husband close on forty years,
and never once endured a serious doubt of it.
You marriage critics, lend your stereo ears;
things must be good in bed; but in or out of it
respectful gentleness is what adheres,
once urgent flesh consumes its passion's rage
if you would keep a glow against cold age.

26

When what's described as peace again returned
a trainee I became in colour printing.
My bosses rationed everything I learned,
at greater speed and riches always hinting.
Dissatisfied with what I did and earned,
I broke from business bonds and set off sprinting
at my own pace up sloping Mount Parnassus.
How fortunate I listen to de Lassus,

27

or once again I'd stumble for a rhyme!
Broadcasting, writing, music-criticising,
and making love and poetry, the time
went quickly by without me realising
how brief the leafing years we call our prime.
In middle age we take to agonising
when fledglings rough us up in raucous tone
no matter what we've done or promise shown;

28

a thing that Scotland's wee-ness makes unique.
You must be useless if they knew your father,
or "kennt yir faither" if in Scots you'd speak,
no longer a rich thoughtful tongue, but rather
a broken *patois* practised by a clique
(it's odd how fact puts some folk in a lather!)
of poetasters who, with nought to say
exhale their feeble breath on its decay.

You'd almost think I thought such nonsense counted!
I knew three poets who could use Scots well.
MacDiarmid, on his wings of genius, mounted
the lyric heights, until he sought to spell
out praise for Communism. Then, much dunted,
his muse excused chopped prose and doggerel.
Who fought to break the Scots parochial cage
supported gunned suppression in old age.

Dear Goodsir Smith, who sang of drink and women,
a connoisseur of laughter, wit and art;
of Scotland's writers warmly the most human,
monied and monocled to play the part:
and Alexander Scott, who right on cue ran
the follies of our land beneath a scart
of witty epigram. But their successors!—
let's call them Lallans Inc., prefixed by Messrs.

A Scottish writer has a choice of tongues—
Scots, Gaelic, English which we mostly speak,
the other two the subject of ding-dongs
through *Scotsman* letters every second week,
as if there was some case of rights and wrongs
that angry argument could win or break.
It's not the tongue that matters, but what's said in it;
unless it's how you feel, you'll be found dead in it.

32

Write English, and they'll say that you're defeatist.
If faced with quality that quite surpasses,
they'll dub your witty imagery élitist
unless it echoes praise for leftish masses,
whose sense of judgement's never been the neatest,
their clichés roaring out like sounding brasses.
Reject such brays with dignified austerity;
true judgement's given only by posterity.

33

Besides, wise living means that when we taste it
we savour each sensation as it offers.
Our circled round's too wonderful to waste it,
however much in thankless youth we're scoffers.
Age fingers time more thinly, and we haste it
unless we linger over all it proffers:
the texture's brittler but the touch more fine,
the flavour summered deeper through the wine.

34

To wine, I must admit, I've long been partial;
our link of bliss with mythic ages gone.
Alas! for those its elixir makes martial;
who drink it, then can't bear to look upon
another without violence; a farce you'll
agree is best avoided, not outshone.
When wine, the gift of light, provokes aggression,
a smalling creature mirrors his recession.

35

It's puzzled me how Scotsmen, wrapped up thickly
in inarticulateness, or when boozy,
fall into forceful argument and quickly
go fucking this and fucking that, their floosy
a naked oath. It makes the sober sickly—
allowing too much drink leaves men less choosey!—
to hear the link of joy that's life's infinity
with violence thus placed in consanguinity.

36

Poor tolerance, a pity you're so boring
that poets never wing you out in odes
or hymns of praise empowered to send you soaring
in strains to deafen all the niggling goads
of anger, setting men and nations roaring
at those who follow unfamiliar codes!
In wordy brawling, whether one's just socked, or
been felled, you wait on call, their only doctor.

37

There's not a man but needs his fill of pleasure
as through this vale of tears he's forced to pedal,
though when he meets with matters he can't measure
his views mean nothing and he'd best not meddle;
yet when he treats of what he loves in leisure,
though other folk might think it fiddle-faddle,
he's found his secret path to human glory,
lending exultant meaning to his story.

Whose story? Once again, my lines have bounded
unfenced from what is meant to be their theme,
the story of my life. So, muse, be rounded
up quietly this purpose to redeem.
When Scotland's television first was founded
the studio lights from many a slanting beam
focused on me, explaining why those japers,
The Jolly Beggars, cut immortal capers.

39

I'd been to see a television high man
to say: *I want to do the TV thing.*
But being an administrative fly-man
he questioned: *What experience do you bring?*
None yet, said I. He sighed and countered: *Why man,
if we want you we'll give your 'phone a ring.*
Experience, I blurted, *comes through function.*
A paradox! he answered, smooth as unction.

40

I fumed and fretted at such bare stupidity,
for double-tongued excuses I abhor;
but he proved innocent of such cupidity.
*To tell the truth I don't put too much store
on Gaelic Mods; but, treated with fluidity,
these Teuchters may not prove too big a bore.
Go up to Oban with a camera crew,*
he said: *and then we'll see what you can do.*

41

So I began my years of interviewing,
a smiling bow-tie image in the box,
trimming the tales of others to my cueing
through subjects sober, gay or heterodox,
the muddied paths of fact and truth pursuing.
Pause now, if you are one of those who mocks
the media. A thirst for information's
a taste that's only quenched in western nations.

42

"Pursuing truth" seems slightly high-faluting!
Of sides, my father claimed, the truth had three;
A's, passionately held, proved convoluting
when laid against the same believed by C.
The third approach, for which there's no one rooting,
passes somewhere between, elusive B.
And yet TV, for all its violent crudity
can sometimes strip a lie to mental nudity.

43

When *What is truth?* impatient Pilate queried
and for an answer would not wait, no wonder.
Since time for us began our wits have wearied
to find it, and we've torn ourselves asunder
quarrelling over rigmaroles that varied
this god from that, and each another blunder;
yet deep in our duplicity there lies
the strange belief there's life beyond the skies.

44

There's instinct in us all to stay alive,
without a struggle never to succumb.
The power at which all holy men connive
wields mindless fear to keep the doubters dumb.
Eternal hope's but brute survival's drive,
and reaches back the dark from which we come.
There's not a word been heard from *there*, outside,
that parsons haven't dreamt, then deified.

45

While chasing such chimeras as we long for,
at least we may establish proven facts,
though rarely what a poet sings his song for.
Gusted by passions, some impromptu acts
until they're over seem worth doing wrong for.
But life's a shifting compromise of pacts;
we sell ourselves to hold defeats at bay
till unexcusing age sweeps all away.

46

Broadcasting kept life filtering through my fingers,
sampling the surface truth of many ways;
yet something of their added substance lingers,
leaving my heart a testament of praise;
not for heroics that Mancunian "sing-gers"
proclaim wherever management best pays;
but hopes and fears expressed in such humility
you'd weep to hear the creak of their fragility.

47

The fame a face attracts is unconvincing,
its partial level cut across the knees.
I've told the young, and watched their inward wincing,
that television's just like canning peas,
or stamping parts in factories, or mincing
up meat for sausages. Neglect to please,
and you'll be superseded in a twinkling,
with not a friend to share your lonely drinking!

48

It's better far to write a single verse
that fifty years from now sets one heart aching
in sympathy with what the lines rehearse,
than share a pop star's psychedelic shaking
of mindless millions; or look out—what's worse?—
to watch your insincerity overtaking;
or find yourself unbuttoning public scandal
to give your name a marketable handle.

49

Some writers have a passion for variety,
claiming it's what our flesh and blood were made for,
the constant repetition of satiety.
But many of the lovelies that get laid for
such pleasures as they lend, find notoriety
a post-coital sadness better paid for;
so, baring grief and naked secrets, sell
their tale of twitchings to the *Sunday Yell*.

50

A lovely woman taking off her clothing's
delight to men; a glimpse of promised seas
to carry freights of bliss and soft supposings,
meeting the distance of a moment's ease.
The eager male, when he begins disposing
of socks and trousers and the need to please
assumes a kind of awkward comicality,
if such things may be judged by rationality.

51

Our sexual tastes come varied, like religion,
and I'm not one to prate morality,
or urge the lusty young to keep the fridge on,
as preachers beg the commonality
with vested interest to preserve a bridge on
the gulf from life to immortality:
but parsons peer through self-deluding mists;
I don't believe a future state exists.

52

Or that a god of any kind's worth knowing
who needs continual praise for what he's gifted,
while ministers remind him what he's doing,
or point direction favours might be shifted
(according to his will, since nothing's owing)
as if, from time to time, omnipotence drifted.
The nameless source of life we call creation's
what artists search for through their own sensations.

53

The public think creation's a commotion
that stirs and stumps us every waking hour
while inspiration's poured out like a lotion,
the frenzied gift of some ethereal power.
If there was much in that romantic notion,
poets would all stay thin, composers sour:
unceasing works of art are indigestible;
we must exist on something more comestible.

54

Reporting rapes and writing up disasters
to poets is a kind of muse-abuse,
and few who do it ever prove long lasters.
On radio and TV, with George Bruce—
our audiences were more discerning masters—
the present and the past we'd introduce,
tracing the settled heritage that shaped us
and probing where its energy escaped us.

55

A shadow that has lost its substance, feeling
as well supported as a verbless clause,
the Scottish spirit's been too long congealing
in banknotes, sour religion and thinned laws,
while round about, the busy world is dealing
in purposes that wear a living cause.
Though Scots pretend they long for devolution,
they vote unchanged the London constitution.

56

That frees them from the burden of decision,
allowing them complain when things go wrong,
noising abroad much paper-dart derision
to keep the fiction jollying along.
No matter how original their vision,
they're soon bought out by foreign firms more strong.
Since most by now accept their branch-line station,
why press dishonoured claims to be a nation?

57

One must stay positive, though Scotland's slipping
beyond retrieval to provincial status;
for what will not return it's no use weeping.
Mankind's long march goes on. It should elate us
that slowly fairer values are outstripping
those with which privilege could still negate us
if democratic rule became dictation,
to tyrant's or Trade Unions' subjugation.

58

It was, perhaps, as wild a piece of dreaming
to visualise a virile Scotland, free
to make its choices, as the thought that scheming
among globe-trotting statesmen could decree
a peaceful balance for the world's redeeming,
the universal, equal vis-à-vis.
Since history's the sum of spent confusion,
all human life must end in disillusion.

59

That need not be depressing if around us
the young, impatient as they watch us fail,
await their turn, from dreaming to confound us
as straightly as a hammer hits the nail.
They'll learn one day, perhaps before they ground us,
that we, too, strove to break that harsh entail
bonded in blood so distant we can't think of it
though nowhere near, as yet, the middle link of it.

60

There was a time I thought my muse forsook me,
her usual urgent voice quite hard to hear;
and much that I then wrote wore such a look, the
reviewers drubbed me for being far from clear.
Five further years of wooing her it took me
before the saucy jade would reappear;
but when she did, at last she hung her hat up,
and here and there some kindly critic sat up.

61

Yet what's a muse but a convention, hoary
with time; a useful way to blame another
should readers much dislike a poem or story.
Some poets find their muse a shrilling bother;
Burns found his Coila such a crashing bore, he
addressed her like some nagging Holy Mother.
Of technique if you've laid a good supply on,
a kind sub-conscious is what you rely on.

62

And yet it's hard to keep a poem in focus,
guiding it towards its proper destination;
with winning words a facile muse provokes us
to jostle like a crammed suburban station;
or vague with dampish sentiment, so soaks us
we're forced to do a drying operation;
destroy what we have laboured at thus vainly
and shape another poem with moves more gainly.

63

Why bother writing poetry? folk ask me
from time to time. *It doesn't make much money.*
Quite true. And shaping verses doesn't bask me
in that enriched acclaim men find most sunny.
The inner voice is urgent, and can task me
to shut myself in my own mental dunny
while others brazen on the frolicked beach
reserved for those whose fortune's in their reach.

64

If human life bears any kind of reason
we're bound to seek whatever we do best
and nourish it through each succeeding season
till both the flower and fruit are manifest.
To kill the gifts we're given is a treason
that never should allow our conscience rest;
nor must we wield the mutilating knife
though fashioned critics make self-doubting rife.

65

Besides, why cramp a poet when he's wound up?
Staccato stammerings in verse called free
are what most would-be versifiers sound up
who pay their own poetic licence fee;
exhausted words and nerveless clichés bound up
for Editors, first class delivery.
So long as I'm a poet in employment,
I see no reason to forgo enjoyment.

66

No more apologies for such digression!
Few lives, thank goodness, ever run to plan.
We're linked by little more than chance succession,
leaving us rearrange as best we can.
Those who believe they've souls maintain confession
disperses faults, like some forgiving fan,
leaving them free to err again tomorrow,
a form of consolation I can't borrow.

67

Life jolts us on. We need to wash our faces
and laugh at times. Mere philosophic platitudes
never excuse us from those daily paces
that mete out disappointments and beatitudes.
Leaving elected men in public places
to strike up further unconvincing attitudes,
we eat, earn, spend, make love and all the rest,
ignore the worst by hoping for the best.

68

I left George Bruce (who made the North-East speak
its poetry of stone) and for a while
towards advertising turned a gentle cheek.
A television station in Carlisle
became my programmed care, and week by week
I broadcast from this city lacking style,
and longed to be in Scotland. I can't think why;
there only were ten English miles to slink by!

69

After six years, patched by an operation,
some programmes worth the doing left behind,
I felt the rub of alien frustration.
Against the English I've no axe to grind,
but when he measures up their education,
it's natural a Scot should have in mind
his children should be taught their own tradition,
however much he views it with suspicion.

70

And I got tired of acting like a Janus,
gazing ahead while glancing to the rear,
a posture that perhaps I should explain thus:
ambition is to TV men a spear
which, stuck in from behind, is sure to pain us,
however much it makes us persevere.
To Scotland I returned, a conservationist
to stem the loss of buildings that the nation missed.

71

To build a city Androcles once planned,
and asked the Delphian oracle where to root it.
While frying fish his soldiers had just panned
a grass fire started. When he tried to put it
out, a wild boar rushed for open land.
The King obeyed instructions. In pursuit it
was slain; Ephesus drawn up, nobly done;
town planning as a discipline begun.

72

Wearing more "hats" than one confuses good folk
(no wonder if bare-headed you keep walking!)
on whom stern duty puts an early rude yoke
that leaves them little room for idle gawking,
whatever doubt some deep instinctual mood spoke.
To multi-coloured Fairbairn I was talking.
Do more than one thing, and they underrate you.
Do just one thing, he answered, *and they'll hate you.*

73

No, not exaggeration: I'm not sneering.
Like animals, our fears are quick to start.
Rub the veneer of speech, you'll find us baring
our claws and teeth, eyes savagely alert;
nations like individuals compeering.
Self-interest commands the leading part
and dominates the nature of our play,
whatever we, or politicians, say.

74

But solaces like poetry and wine,
a loving wife and happy family,
make us to quick forgetfulness incline;
while music lends familiarity
with the rich world of feeling and design
that shapes and keeps its own finality;
such are the only substances we're given
to fill the framework of imagined heaven.

75

I've had my share; of poets known a handful—
Norman MacCaig, Mackay Brown, Crichton Smith—
a friend each with his own poetic brand full
of what makes up a sense of place; the pith
of ancient contrasts such as keeps our land full
of differences, kin without the kith:
a land where Viking, Lowlander and Gael
are unified by name, to no avail.

76

Yet sense of place is nothing, lacking man.
The wilderness would bore beyond belief
were it not measured up within the span
of cultivation's narrowing relief,
reminding us though we both need and can
escape from others briefly, held in fief
of such intelligence as we possess
it's we who clothe the world in meaning's dress.

But there's a quality I'm always careful
of humanising since our basset-hound,
an expert starer-up at you, eyes prayerful,
the laureate of basset-nature found
in Edwin Morgan. Meaning by the lairful
from foreign poets' language he unbound;
wit and compassion matched in like ability,
the voice of an uncommon versatility.

78

I've taken tea with Eliot; with MacNeice
gone drinking, puzzled why his Celtic gloom
and hectic laughter never seemed to piece
together; heard Day Lewis fill a room
with spoken music, lending verse a lease
of life its silent merits don't assume;
talked music and had lunch with E. M. Forster
at Edinburgh and (oh yes!) in Gloucester.

79

I saw in London fragile Richard Strauss,
the last great master who could shake the heart
with ecstasy, before a cheering house
acknowledge its applause, turn and depart,
leaving our sad and bitter times to douse
that finished beauty for the stringent art
of Shostakovitch, irony and power
in music that outlived a tyrant's hour.

For him, like Strauss, it was the world's ear
that listened, then the ear of time itself,
reflecting the anxiety and fear
that keeps afloat our age of measured wealth,
where semi-cloistered Britten let us hear
his half of life. On many a college shelf
dust gathers on the scores of played-once prizes
while silence wipes out aleatoric noises.

81

Francis George Scott, compared with Strauss no master
(what stanza could contain Scott's boisterous roaring!)
and yet of Scottish song a gifted caster,
into a few his Border genius pouring;
a music Scotland had allowed flow past her
soundless since Knox began his graceless goring:
Scott of the chiselled head, poetic teacher
lacking tradition's prop, an under-reacher.

82

Fine painters, too, I've numbered with my friends:
Anne Redpath, swirling poet of soft tones;
MacTaggart, whose romantic landscape blends
the sadness of spent evenings with lost dawns;
and Philipson, whose darting knife portends
the church's empty grandeur and the throne's,
strings fighting cocks with muscle, meditates
the shapes of love, the shadows of its hates.

83

Alas! the fate of most art is to stay put
where it began, and soon be quite forgotten.
But come to that, few people can uproot
themselves to move from where they were begotten;
when travel's cheap, their poverty's acute,
or some dictator simply says: *It's not on*.
So I've been lucky, able to enjoy
much travel. It's the little things annoy.

84

For instance, go to Italy or Spain
in the high season with a mob of British;
so constantly and rudely they'll complain,
your patience and your teeth will soon be grit-ish;
you'll wonder why they pay to buy such pain.
The life-and-soul-of-party ones grow skittish;
others want fish-and-chips and English telly,
declaring foreign drains are always smelly.

85

I like to travel with my wife alone
and let myself absorb the atmosphere;
those sights and sounds and scents together grown
that make an ancient place uniquely *here*;
what neither time nor wars have overthrown,
I like to view the gracious and the rare,
and celebrate in thankful meditation
such triumphs over much abomination.

86

It's not that I abhor my fellow men—
I loathe the stuck-up and the hoity-toity—
but long before a poet lifts his pen
his pregnant muse must keep her own society.
It's only through what swims into his ken
a writing man can add his little moiety
to that great store of what we all inherit,
from which we take more than we give, or merit.

87

Now that the world's afflictions reach us nightly
inside our homes, our minds erect protection
against such constant horror, brushing lightly
past conscience. Those who, by their own election,
devote their days to charity, and brightly
attempt to make some limited correction
find that like waves the poor come on; too many
not bettered by the billionth of a penny.

88

My wife in Turkey, eating shiskebab,
was stared at by a mangy prowling cat.
She threw it a small scrap. With a lean grab
it gulped it down. At once, from nowhere, pat
on cue, more cats appeared, each one a dab
at woeful staring, till a dozen sat
around her, ownerless and underfed.
For starving Turkish catdom her heart bled.

89

What's to be done? Keep down the population
of Turkish cats, or change the Turkish nature?
Or cultivate a sensitive frustration
that Asiatic cats must face a fate your
best friend would not wish on his worst relation?
Or, like some dotty Englishwoman, sate your
distress by feeding cats in countless numbers;
so that, though millions starve, your conscience slumbers?

90

Guiltily I admire the dedication
of those who use their strength against the leak
of bursting life that's born to face starvation,
its fate a listless year or two to eke
existence scratched from penny-pinched donation,
of which the gods of ignorance never speak.
But like all else, denial's a vocation
that finds its bleak reward, self-contemplation.

91

I'm conscious of the useless contribution
a symphony, a poem or picture makes;
but mankind's ache of ills wears no solution;
one trouble cured, and out another breaks.
Not even wisdom patiently Confucian
can feed the starving, heal the blood that cakes
on innocence, the always-losing side
in lying wars by dogma deified.

92

But numbers never multiply intensity;
a single victim knows the most of pain.
Though sprawling millions suffer, the immensity
is that one pattern over and again.
Our joy and sorrow's limited in density
it can't exceed, however much we'd fain
carry a broader burden. Thus denied,
the Christian myth needs Jesus crucified.

93

So art's the one resource an individual
can use to purify that sense of guilt
round each and every one of us decidual,
yet not be lured into the fatal silt
of shining superstitions, the residual—
so thickly spread, so generously spilt—
of status-seeking cruelties and lusts
religions use to prop their painted crusts.

94

Enough of that! It's through their own abstractions
the Scots get bogged and sink what's plain lucidity
with metaphysics' substitute for actions,
a devious disguise for hard cupidity.
I've had no time for party, clique or faction;
my constant search has always been for quiddity.
When properly grown tired of studying Man,
not God but earth, the healer's, what I scan.

95

My richest years were spent in Gartocharn;
Loch Lomond jagging distance blue with hills
endlessly ripping clouds that winds re-darn,
and gathering burns from winter's former chills.
Down battered rock and brackened ridge they churn,
hanging a silence white on distant rills,
shouldering thickened valleys far below,
their journey's breathing born of frozen snow.

96

The River Endrick, by whose whorling bank
we picnicked, sunned and sported summer days,
relaxed, gave up its surging pools and shrank,
a glitter threading fields of yellow haze
where, as we swam or splashed some children's prank,
we'd feel the flick of passing salmon graze
ankle or leg, our sense of apprehension
the mountained surface of the water's tension.

97

Riding the moorland, cantering the strand,
or fording, horses breast-high, streams and rivers,
we were a lazy motley-mounted band,
not dressed to kill, like hunting's easy-livers;
as happy fronting rain as in the bland
warmth of the sun, or moving through the shivers
of mountain valleys, silently alarming,
where summer's greening truce brings no disarming.

98

New neighbours born of ballads in the Borders,
grew passionate about their rolling acres,
where still they grouped inside their feudal orders.
Of tally-ho-ing we were not partakers,
of breeding bloodstock, never near afforders,
of riding, dear and formal, thus forsakers,
preferring over Annan's banks to roam,
its waters flowing past our Georgian home.

99

Three years I spent in Cumbria; Head's Nook
a shipping tycoon chose for his retreat,
leaving a village sounding like a joke
first built to serve his neo-Gothic seat.
We lived above a wooded glen. A brook
rehearsed beneath our windows its conceit
shrugged from the distant Pennines, whose cold range
gives England's east and west their interchange.

100

A terraced house in Greek Victorian style
brought our return to Glasgow, where the pace
of life had slackened; pile on crumbling pile
of tenements that once had housed a race
of purpose change had failed to reconcile,
bulldozed and cleared to leave uneven space;
its empty-handed workers gone, or slunk
into their own despair, its purpose shrunk.

101

All of us love the place of our nativity,
an instinct that we share with eels and salmon;
whether by wars or crime locked in captivity
or merely kept abroad through serving Mammon,
in youth's broad plains or age's steep declivity
the one affection that we rarely sham on.
Glasgow, it makes me sad to see how tumbled
your worldly image is, your influence crumbled!

102

For you have streets and terraces as splendid
as anything that Europe could produce
and—better late than never—you've expended
much conservation effort to induce
your golden stone to gleam as first intended.
Although it makes some Edinburgers puce
to hear it, your Victorian effulgence
no longer needs their Georgian indulgence.

103

What's gone for ever is the racing surge
of Glasgow feeling. It survived the slums,
a blunt alertness, its own end and urge,
reeking togetherness like clarty lums.
It's swept away with deprivation's scourge,
not showing up on screened computers' sums.
To say such things makes planners grow dyspeptic;
at least their Glasgow's much more antiseptic.

104

In cities, as in states, affairs of gravity
too often leave poor commonsense in tatters,
the public weal abandoned in some cavity
exposed when party dogma's all that matters.
Then, no amount of politicians' suavity
can heal the damage prejudice thus shatters:
we vote down leaders, raise the opposition
to find we haven't varied our condition.

105

However much we rage at the confusion
that clogs our wheeled economy, the fact is
the dream of faultless order's an illusion.
At least the muddled freedom we enact is
more pleasant than dictatorship's obtrusion,
when individuals find the social pact is:
Believe just what you're told, or be suppressed;
the State's the ultimate good; the State knows best.

106

How easily such generalities
blow up when near to politics we're veering!
It's only those who practise caring qualities
achieved by piecemeal social engineering,
and use the hard-won vague formalities
democracy depends on, should be steering
the ship of state; that leaky, lumbering boat
that, come what may, must keep us all afloat.

107

Though frail democracy has never ceased
breathing its message to whatever tongue
the rights of human liberty are leased,
there's no belief that flaunted time's not flung
to fragments, its accepted spells released
for scholars of dry death to nose among,
and marvel how credulity held charms
to shield against mortality's alarms.

108

Beware of him applauded on a rostrum
naïve with self-conceit that fortifies,
who claims he's found the one sure-curing nostrum,
fanaticism voltaging his eyes.
His remedy must prove a postulatum
of worn-out dogma decked in weak surmise.
It doesn't matter whose the hand that shoots:
you're dead. But life holds no such absolutes.

109

Having lived through the world's worst yet convulsion
and watched it heal the wounds and struggle towards
a kind of peace that holds its own compulsion,
nuclear horror checking savage hordes
who'd sweep through Europe but for this repulsion,
with anger I reject the traitorous words
of those who claim vast armies mean no harm,
for meek example bid the rest disarm.

110

In continents of envy, men not greatly
unlike ourselves sit planning our destruction,
forcing us match their weapons, hoping straightly
such tit-for-tat may prompt the sane deduction:
should either side attack, then desperately
both will go down through one atomic suction;
what man has fashioned through ten thousand years
annihilated; atavistic fears

111

that once he ranged pre-history with, prove stronger
than all he gained through his inquiring mind,
his reasoned, civilising values wrong; or
not sure enough to shape what they defined.
A sterile earth's swirled gases aeons longer
than luckless man's pathetic, glorious kind;
and could again revolve such timeless slack,
the human burden shaken off its back.

112

Those cushioned strategists who think that killings's
inevitable—quite a noble pastime—
charged up with threats and platitudes, seem willing
to kid themselves that life beyond the blast time
would still go on; that no atomic grilling
could ever truly prove a human last time.
Some might survive, to animals mutated:
it's peaceful life we want perpetuated.

113

Even now there's power deployed ten times too much
to still the world, kill everything that moved.
Whose finger might provide destruction's touch?
And if it did so, what would it have proved?
The fearful curse of human power is such
it digs itself a rut so deeply grooved
that source and purpose are alike forgot,
and all must be possessable—or nought!

114

Such scaring matters easily depress us;
might seem, perhaps too serious for versing.
Not priests but poets sometimes best confess us,
give balance, sending warning-clouds dispersing.
There's Nature's here-and-now around to bless us,
discharging might-have-beens from needless nursing,
reminding us we aren't too meticulous
thinking self-frightened death a whit ridiculous.

115

To give much thought to might-have-beens is folly,
yet sometimes I regret my stubborn knees
could never make of Christmas more than holly,
the celebration when we try to please,
the time that shops relieve us of our lolly
as conscience gets no cheaper to appease.
How comfortable thinking you're aware of
a faith that mean *Forever's* taken care of!

116

The more so since on hills that claim St. Patrick
(though doubtless he was born on Irish soil)
I live, a superstition-cured agnostic
(St. Peter, you can put that on your file!)
creature of Europe's culture, mainly Catholic,
its flower, delight, though nurtured in old guile.
Which goes to prove that pleasures rarely come
without some shadowed pain's residuum.

117

I look across the silver-threaded Clyde,
its summer banks a gleam of banding copper
doused grey beneath each spilling of the tide.
The water flecks and flees, a running chopper
abrupt with winter into which a slide
of mountain thick with storm can't put a stopper;
trees creak; the whole house whistles disarray.
Our guests admire the view, though, either way.

118

Here, in old age, I mock pontificators
in titled jobs of which they're briefly holders,
secured by Commons privilege or gaiters,
who, warning us of pebbles, trip on boulders;
Trade Union bullies, marching nuclear praters
(a clutch of waiting antis in their folders)
while millions suffer since the words most needed
are nowhere said; or, hinted at, unheeded.

119

In poetry, warned Shelley, don't embody
of right and wrong your own time-bound conception;
(although to some it seems a trifle odd he
so frequently allowed himself exception).
It is, indeed, a self-inflicted rod, the
too frequent use of which meets rough reception
from those who love to show off in a naughty pose,
yet think poetic moralising otiose.

120

Much verse I've written of the kind called heavy,
but now, however shrill the critics rage—
MacIncomplete, Courageous and the bevy
round Grecian Glen, or Portobello's sage—
I've done with paying up ambition's levy,
am quite without desire to be a mage;
so laugh where once I wept, and choose to write
a kind of verse indubitably light.

121

Auden proclaimed no poem he had written
had saved a single Jew from being gassed.
If he had hoped to do so, then he'd bitten
off more than art can chew, and was surpassed
by the great Christian God who chose to sit on
his silence while by thousands Jews were massed,
allowing man to exercise free will
doing the things he's best at; starve and kill.

122

They'd disagree who think the world is running
to some celestial plan, and so has meaning,
a viewpoint I've no difficulty shunning.
I can't believe in fate whose ravelled skeining
is changed by trivial chance and mindless gunning.
The earth, I think's, an accident, careening
through time and space whose stuff we can't conceive,
indifferent to everything we cleave.

123

Those stars that mariners thought everlasting
splutter to cinders through the dark they lace;
the silver moon has no more spells for casting
since astronauts have bounced upon her face;
the cloth of heaven, its white-robed saints repasting
while angels harp, lies crumpled in disgrace:
Eternity's not there for our alighting;
it's cosmic junk that rocket probes are sighting.

124

To find ourselves, however accidental,
alive, enjoying children, Mozart, wine,
such countless pleasures, bodily and mental,
as we are given to pass along the line
here in a world to which we owe no rental,
one sexing link in nature's close design,
is wonderful enough without obtaining
a *why* and *wherefore* which there's no explaining.

125

Through grandchildren we see our hopes projected
just when we feel that soon we'll be disbanded;
their mix of genes, by chance and love selected,
two pasts reshuffled, dealing single-handed
whatever cards heredity's elected
(though fortunately can't yet be commanded)
to play another spanning of the game
of human life with, never twice the same.

126

Ahead, there's darkness. Death comes as the end.
Of this we have as little right complaining
as not possessing centuries to spend,
or lining up to watch Rome's legions training
or having Willie Shakespeare for a friend.
The universe in all its wide sustaining
will fall, they say, into a final black hole,
succeeded then by nothingness's slack whole.

127

As years pile up their tiny little load, a
man feels his strength and faculties declining.
Since I'll not be around to write a coda
(dear reader, don't pretent that you're repining!)
I'll pour myself a whisky dashed with soda
and draw one last conclusive underlining—
Farewell, my muse! For you, my darling wife,
and everything you gave us, thank you, life!

NOTES ON A NET TO CATCH THE WINDS

Stanza 5 Sir Compton Mackenzie claimed to have the gift of total recall from the age of two. His autobiographical *Octaves* abound in examples. In October 1947 he came to lunch with my wife and me, along with C. M. Grieve ("Hugh MacDiarmid"), Professor John Glaister, the forensic expert, and the Reverend H. S. Maclelland, the actor-manqué minister of Trinity Church (now the Henry Wood S.N.O. Centre) in Claremont Street. My wife elected to serve fish, but a storm at sea had delayed deliveries to the shops. During the soup course, while my wife was trying to advance things in the kitchen, Mackenzie, deep in anecdotal reminiscence, picked up the fish server instead of his spoon and plunged it into the soup. Soup spattered in all directions through the decorative holes. "Ah! A social error," said Mackenzie, wiping the server on his napkin, and picking up his story in mid-sentence.

More than thirty years later, in conversation with my wife, he recalled the occasion, the trivial incident and the exact details of the location of our flat in Southpark Avenue, Glasgow, to which this was his only visit.

Stanza 29 MacDiarmid publicly supported the Russian armed interventions in Hungary and Czechoslovakia, acts of aggression that disgusted the Free World.

Stanza 30 Sadly, the Scots tongue has steadily declined under the relentless pressures of cinema, radio and television. While it has certainly been a long time in dying, the erosion of its individual words, leaving behind only English words pronounced in a dialect manner, does not augur well for its future as a fruitful medium for creative writing.

Stanza 72 Nicholas Fairbairn, Q.C., whose original and colourful garb and forthright opinions made him a noted

63

figure even before he became a Member of Parliament and in Mrs. Thatcher's Government Solicitor General for Scotland. In *Thomas Campion: Poet, Composer and Physician* (1970); Lowbury, Salter and Young remark: "In contrast with the Renaissance ideal of the balanced man who aspired to do all things well, the ideal cultivated in the nineteenth and twentieth centuries has been specialist and monolithic; hence a distrust of the varied talents of the 'Jack-of-all-trades'."

Stanza 77 See Edwin Morgan's poem "An Addition to the Family". Although the poet got to know my basset-hound, Hector (and Toby, his successor), the story of my double interest in basset-horns and basset-hounds, the basis of the poem, was told to Morgan by George Bruce before Morgan met the animal.

Stanza 79 At the Edinburgh International Festival and the Three Choirs Festival.

Stanza 80 The reference is to Sir Karl Popper's theory (in *Unended Quest*) that great art exists in "world 3" as distinct from things ("world 1") or our subjective interpretation of them ("world 2").

Stanza 81 Francis George Scott was not only the English teacher of the boy C. M. Grieve (Hugh MacDiarmid) at a Langholm school, but a perceptive and instructive critic to many late Scots poets. (c.f. my *Francis George Scott and the Scottish Renaissance* [1980].)

Stanza 106 "piecemeal social engineering". The phrase is Popper's.

Stanza 120 Lorn MacIntyre, Alan Bold, Duncan Glen (towards none of whom I bear any malice) and Tom Scott, whose many letters to *The Scotsman* have included the suggestion that Hugh MacDiarmid might be commemorated by the establishment of a Bardic College.